FAMILIAR JOURNEY

FAMILIAR JOURNEY

Poems
by
Peggy Pond Church

New Foreword
by
Peter Deckert

SOUTHWEST HERITAGE SERIES

SUNSTONE
PRESS

SANTA FE

No part of this book may be reproduced in any form or by any electronic or
mechanical means including information storage and retrieval systems
without permission in writing from the publisher, except by a reviewer
who may quote brief passages in a review.

Sunstone books may be purchased for educational, business, or sales promotional use.
For information please write: Special Markets Department, Sunstone Press,
P.O. Box 2321, Santa Fe, New Mexico 87504-2321.

Printed on acid-free paper
∞

Library of Congress Cataloging-in-Publication Data

Church, Peggy Pond, 1903-1986.
  [Poems. Selections]
  Familiar journey : poems / by Peggy Pond Church.
    pages cm. -- (Southwest Heritage Series)
  "New Foreword by Peter Deckert."
  ISBN 978-0-86534-134-0 (softcover : alk. paper)
  I. Title.
  PS3505.H946F3 2014
  811'.52--dc23
                        2013045655

WWW.SUNSTONEPRESS.COM
SUNSTONE PRESS / POST OFFICE BOX 2321 / SANTA FE, NM 87504-2321 /USA
(505) 988-4418 / ORDERS ONLY (800) 243-5644 / FAX (505) 988-1025

CONTENTS

SOUTHWEST HERITAGE SERIES

I

THE SOUTHWEST HERITAGE SERIES

"The past is not dead. In fact, it's not even past."
—William Faulkner, *Requiem for a Nun*

The history of the United States is written in hundreds of regional histories and literary works. Those letters, essays, memoirs, biographies and even collections of fiction are often first-hand accounts by people who wanted to memorialize an event, a person or simply record for posterity the concerns and issues of the times. Many of these accounts have been lost, destroyed or overlooked. Some are in private or public collections but deemed to be in too fragile condition to permit handling by contemporary readers and researchers.

However, now with the application of twenty-first century technology, nineteenth and twentieth century material can be reprinted and made accessible to the general public. These early writings are the DNA of our history and culture and are essential to understanding the present in terms of the past.

The Southwest Heritage Series is a form of literary preservation. Heritage by definition implies legacy and these early works are our legacy from those who have gone before us. To properly present and preserve that legacy, no changes in style or contents have been made. The material reprinted stands on its own as it first appeared. The point of view is that of the author and the era in which he or she lived. We would not expect photographs of people from the past to be re-imaged with modern clothes, hair styles and backgrounds. We should not, therefore, expect their ideas and personal philosophies to reflect our modern concepts.

Remember, reading their words and sharing their thoughts is a passport back into understanding how the past was shaped and how it influenced today's world.

Our hope is that new access to these older books will provide readers with a challenging and exciting experience.

PEGGY POND CHURCH

II

FOREWORD
to
This Edition
by
Peter Dechert

We found life is not what we dream but something that dreams us.
—Peggy Pond Church, "Letter to Virginia"

Some poets create transparent poems. Others create opaque poems.

By this, I mean that one can see through transparent poems to the poets themselves, but one catches few glimpses of the poets behind opaque poems. Opaque poems are not necessarily hard to understand: if you have a year or so to spare for the task, read through Longfellow's collected works. You'll understand just about all of them, but you'll also come away with very little perception of just what sort of a real person Longfellow was. His poetry is opaque simply because he did not put much of himself into what he wrote.

Another variety of opaque poems is those whose actual meaning seems to be unclear, for example Ezra Pound's "Cantos." In these cases, we seem to see the poet struggling to express ideas that he himself had not yet fully apprehended: the reader may decide that the poet had bitten off more than he could chew, could not digest it, could not fully transmit himself or his ideas to the reader because he was unsure just who "himself" or what "his ideas" might be.

Peggy Pond Church was active during a time frame within which hindsight suggests the latter sort of opacity seemed to predominate. Scholars were citing works by Pound, T. S. Eliot, Wallace Stevens, William Carlos Williams, and others like them as being models of "avant-garde" poetic construction. Most critics seemed to think during the middle years of the twentieth century that poets had to tackle difficult, obscure subjects aggressively in order to be worthy of serious consideration, even if they never reached satisfactory resolutions.

Robert Frost probably came closer than any of Peggy's contemporaries to breaking this trend in scholarly judgment. He occupied a sort of middle ground: on the scale I have suggested, we might call Frost a translucent poet. He was essentially objective: we could understand his poems, but not always be quite sure where he himself stood in relation to a number of them. Were they simply observations, or did they reflect firmly held convictions, basic beliefs?

Peggy made transparent poems.

Reading Peggy's poems today, we realize that we are immediately, even intimately, in touch with Peggy herself. In a very real sense, Peggy's poems were, and still are, Peggy. We discover Peggy through them. They were created out of her convictions, convictions that she was able to translate into meaningful words, phrases, sentences: entities. Created, too, out of her emotions. She had no hesitation when it came to tackling difficult subjects, nor any fear of facing her subject matter head-on. And once she had made her poem, no reader could doubt that he had been spoken to by a real person, wholly involved.

My acquaintance with Peggy went through two phases, with an interval of almost thirty years. The first phase was during my two years at the Los Alamos Ranch School, from which I graduated in 1941. Fermor Church, Peggy's husband, known universally to his friends as "Ferm," was our Assistant Headmaster and principal science teacher. Peggy, it seems to me, was our principal iconoclast.

Peggy's father, Ashley Pond Jr., started a guest ranch on the Pajarito Plateau about 1912; in 1917 he founded what was at first a sort of recuperative facility, largely for boys from the east who had become ill; this facility had developed into the Ranch School twenty-two years before I arrived in 1939. Thus, as a youngster, Peggy spent formative years in the mesa and mountain country on the Plateau; she quickly grew to love it. And she explored it thoroughly both then and later, on horseback, on foot, climbing—and no doubt sometimes falling.

Pond, a concept person, not an educator, employed A. J. Connell to be the School's "Director" almost immediately after it was established. Connell, born in New York City, came to Pond's attention when he was reassigned to Santa Fe in 1914, after having been in the Forest Service in Silver City, New Mexico; he was an enthusiastic Boy Scout leader as well as a Forest Ranger in both locations. Like Pond, Connell had had no experience as an academic educator, and in fact had never been to college. His goal in the beginning was to train the boys to be at the same time obedient and independent: ultimately self-sufficient within any set of circumstances. This goal was totally in accord with Pond's own concept for the school. Pond left the Ranch School in Connell's hands in 1917 in order to try to become an army pilot in San Diego. When he returned to New Mexico, it was to live in Santa Fe, not at Los Alamos.

In 1918, after the School's first year, "AJ" (a universally applied nickname, though he was also called by students "The Boss" behind his back) hired Fayette Curtis to oversee the formal education process, and devoted himself to training his boys to handle their lives within this environment. He retained final control, however, over everything that happened on the Ranch.

Ferm Church arrived at the School from Harvard a few years later. He and Peggy fell in love and were married in 1924, after she had spent two years at Smith College. AJ had many prejudices, among which was a disapproval of employing married teachers to live at the School with their wives. But Peggy was Ashley Pond's daughter, and AJ had to make the best of it and put up with the situation. Peggy, as independent a soul as ever was, insisted on going her own way instead of bowing to AJ's expectations for the behavior of a Master's wife; the result was mutual antipathy that only increased with the years that followed. I recall sitting in classes some mornings and, on looking out the window, seeing Peggy riding into distances all her own, galloping the hum-drum of the School away in search of her personal freedom. Then, I envied her.

By the later 1930s, ten years after L. S. Hitchcock became Headmaster following Curtis's death, the School had been further revamped, with increased emphasis on the academic area. By then, too, it had become the custom at dinner for Masters to preside over most of the tables for six at which we ate in the Fuller Lodge, and if a Master was married (as happened increasingly in later years, AJ's prejudice notwithstanding) his wife was supposed to sit at the foot of his table. Peggy avoided this task at every opportunity. She did, after all, have three sons to raise; but by the time I came to Los Alamos they were old enough to take care of themselves. Two, indeed, were enrolled as students. No matter, it is a fact that we saw less of Peggy than of any other wife, though she did seem to enjoy helping to coach us in the annual Gilbert and Sullivan operettas that we learned to perform.

It remains a wonder to me that my copy of *Foretaste* was inscribed to me personally by Peggy on the day of my graduation. I have it still, of course.

Almost three decades later my wife and I and our three daughters moved permanently here to Santa Fe. Following several years in Taos, where in 1944 Fermor had tried unsuccessfully to reestablish the Ranch School a year and a half after the government had commandeered the area that was centered on the original school site, he and Peggy moved to Berkeley; but by the time my family and I arrived they had moved back to live in Santa Fe. I looked them up. Though they were a generation older than we, we formed a comfortable friendship, visiting each other for meals and talking about the almost always astounding current developments that surface in Santa Fe. After Ferm died in 1975, we still visited with Peggy from time to time, until our own several involvements in Santa Fe's community concerns began to take center stage in our lives, while Peggy herself seemed to grow even more intensely private than she had used to be. She was, although we did not realize it then, working at putting together her final volumes of poetry.

In all our conversations, I do not remember ever having discussed poetry with Peggy: hers or anyone else's. In 1969 I was asked to become the "Founding President" of the New Mexico Poetry Society through a series of laughable errors. I also resumed making some poems of my own. But I cannot recall having even mentioned this fact to her. I guess I instinctively realized that Peggy was concerned with doing poetry, not talking poetry.

Now, a special problem intervenes when it comes to reading "transparent" poems: if the poet is engaged with the topic of her poem to the point of being preoccupied with it, the result may be a number of poems on the same theme, expressing essentially identical points of view. It is hard to read a group of them consecutively without being numbed by the experience. Thus, for example, almost all but the final few poems in Peggy's *Ultimatum for Man* become a real struggle for the reader who elects to take them at a single sitting. She felt passionately about the ruinous effects of World War II on boys-become-soldiers; passionately about the advent of atomic war, about what she saw as the probable demise of civilization and the entire apparently bleak future for mankind—including, far from least, her own sons. Any one or two of these poems taken by itself is impressive, but the totality of all of them experienced at once leaves the reader with a somewhat bitter taste of overkill.

Something like this is also true with the poems that she published about her marriage. She and Ferm were as different as two folk in love could possibly be. Ferm was the practical, down-to-earth scientist and technician personified, concerned with the here, the now, the facts of whatever matter he was investigating. Peggy was the dreamer, in a sense the philosopher, concerned with the myriad possible outcomes rather than the dollars-and-cents sort of single resolution that Ferm had been trained to seek. In a poem celebrating their fortieth wedding anniversary, Peggy expressed their dilemma in these words:

"I like exploring things.
You like knowing what they are made of."

These very different outlooks appear on reading Peggy's poems to have led to some bleak interludes in their long life together, first explored by Peggy in Part I of *Familiar Journey* (1936). The poetic sequence here begins with happiness, travels through turmoil and travail, suggests a short-lived resolution, and ends with something approaching despair, reflecting the actual events of her personal life and hospitalization. But if there was one thing Peggy knew, it was that no matter the differences in their perceptions, she could always count on Ferm to be there for her in his own way.

This never-quite-resolved difference in outlooks forms the entire corpus of *The Ripened Fields: Fifteen Sonnets of a Marriage*, published following Ferm's death forty years after *Familiar Journey* appeared. The final sonnet, indeed, was written for Ferm posthumously; but the other fourteen, quite different in style from the one that ends the collection, are said to have been written much earlier, between 1943 and 1953. As a matter of fact, Part I of *Familiar Journey* incorporates seven sonnets (including the dedicatory one) written in the very same tone and style found in the first fourteen sonnets of *The Ripened Fields*. Since *Familiar Journey* was released in 1936, I believe that all these sonnets, as well as other poems in the same vein, suggest that it took a long while before resolution finally came as the result of having shared and finally melded two lifetimes of outlook and experience.

What is worthy of note in all this, however, is that Peggy never blamed Ferm for being who he was: she blamed herself for not being able to be someone who she wasn't. And all I can add is that, when we renewed our acquaintance in 1969, I saw no signs of any sort of stress between Peggy and Ferm. They were happy together.

Their personal history does not really matter now, nor to us. The only reason I have brought it up is to show a second instance in which, if you read all the pertinent poems at one or two sittings, their totality may become overwhelming: Peggy may perhaps have sometimes created too many variations on a single theme. Poets who hold passionate convictions often do so.

Many of us, as we travel, come upon a scene that particularly attracts us. If we are carrying a camera we may photograph what we see so that we will be able to recall it in years to come. We make its image. Peggy also saw the landscape about her as she walked, rode, and drove through New Mexico's mountains, mesas, and canyons. But she was gifted with a very special ability to add her imagination to the simple image. She saw her surroundings not only as they existed at the moment, but as they might exist in other moments, under different conditions of weather, with other birds in the trees, or with the older cliff-dwelling people still active around them. These special insights illuminate her poems: Peggy seeing things in ways that more mundane folk are not fitted to recognize or record.

No sensitive reader should ever sit down to read a volume of poetry all at once, not even volumes as short as Peggy's are. Each poem worth its salt should be considered and reconsidered before one moves on to the next one, and three or four at one sitting is really a temporary surfeit. Do not sit down to browse through a book of Peggy's poems, short as it may seem: what you hold in your hand is an important fraction of the labor of seventy-odd years.

Truly, Peggy did see not only the things that the rest of us see, but saw them as they may once have been and as they may someday be. All at once. She often saw totality. The poems in the second part of *Familiar Journey* are superb, to choose just one set of examples from amongst them all. And through these transparent poems, we see Peggy herself, a lyric poet of subtle nobility. Her work deserves our notice: everyone's notice.

III

REVIEW

The New Mexico Quarterly, February, 1937, Volume VII, Number 1

Familiar Journey—Peggy Pond Church—Writers' Editions,
Santa Fe, 1936—$2.50.

In this, her second volume of poetry, Peggy Pond Church pursues the course indicated in *Foretaste* published in 1933.

In *Familiar Journey* there is the same dark feminine principle further amplified in this collection of personal lyrics. Both the title poem and the rest of the contents show the author's progress along the road all must travel. It is to be questioned if most of these poems will have a wide appeal, but there is little doubt that those who think and feel as the author does will read the volume with comprehension and esthetic pleasure.

Shelley, in his *Defense of Poetry* has said that a poem is the reflected image of a pleasurable impression upon the imagination; it is the trembling and sounding of the lyre after the wind dies away. As the imaginative mind acts upon its thoughts and experiences, coloring them with its own light and composing from them other thoughts, each containing within itself the principle of its own integrity, thus is a poem written.

Its appeal will be widespread or narrow, based upon the type of imagination of the poet. His personal approach may be so universal, and his skill in expressing it so great, that the reader derives an intenser and purer pleasure through the recognition of kinship to his own emotions than through his own expression.

Most of the images used in these poems are nature images; most of them are keen and sharp and freshly worded, signifying an observance of the small things of nature. Perhaps not always new, they are individual, accurate and vivid.

In the group of poems written about her children, Mrs. Church's phrasing is felicitous, and in these her personal lyric voice becomes universal.

Rarely, too, will be found the sheer poetry which is in "Christ's Birthday." The utter simplicity of phrase, coupled with the strength and delicacy of imagery, in this one poem make it the most remarkable of the contents of the volume. Here is pure rightness of word; pure beauty of image.

> "God is a baby
> needing His mother"

has rare and perfect simplicity.

The final stanzas of this poem, too, illustrate Mrs. Church's observance of the small things of nature:

> "a cool smooth twig
> from the wild choke-cherry,
> and the velvet sheen
> on a juniper berry."

Certain mannerisms detract somewhat from the book as a whole; specifically, the habit of beginning so many of the poems and the stanzas within them with "And."

A certain tendency to invest nature with emotions attributable only to man is noticed; a habit of thought which Ruskin calls "the pathetic fallacy" detracts somewhat from the strength of the other poems in the volume.

—Irene Fisher

IV

OBITUARIES

Santa Fe Style, November 19, 1986
Peggy Pond Church
by
Geoff Gorman

In 1942 Peggy Pond Church found herself at the center of two worlds changing: The Old West outpost of Los Alamos where she had grown up was suddenly taken over by the United States government for the Manhattan Project to develop the atomic bomb. Her coming down from the mesas and canyons of the formerly unknown village on Pajarito Plateau was a journey that took the rest of her life.

For most of the years of her life, Church was a writer. And in her prose and poetry she explored the once-sacred world of the Indians on her familiar mesas and the encroachment by the government, which was to produce there the most powerful instrument of destruction that the world had ever known. Hers was a voice of outrage at one time, but later, through her poetry, she came to be reconciled to what fate had chosen for her beloved land.

Church died on Thursday, Oct. 23, apparently by suicide, at her apartment in a retirement complex in Santa Fe. Some persons close to her said that she had become increasingly despondent over the infirmities of old age, and ended her life by taking a lethal dose of drugs. She was 82 years old.

Her first poem was written when she was only a child, and her last book of poetry, "Birds of Daybreak: Landscapes and Elegies," was published just last year. But Church is perhaps most widely known for her book "The House at Otowi Bridge," published in 1960, in which through recollections of her former neighbor Edith Warner she contrasts the land that she loved as a young girl with the changes brought to Los Alamos by the coming of the nuclear scientists in the early 1940s.

She was born on Dec. 1, 1903, near Watrous, N.M., to Ashley Pond Jr.

and Hazel Hallett Pond. She had a younger brother who died several years ago and a sister who lives in Oregon.

Most of her childhood was spent on Pajarito Plateau where her father built the Los Alamos Ranch School in 1917. Growing up in the Jemez Mountains, the youngster often roamed the nearby mesas and canyons on horseback, learning to appreciate the wilderness setting.

By the age of 11 she had written her first poem, and while she was in high school one of her short stories won $50 in a student competition offered by the Atlantic Monthly.

At an early age she was known for her wonderful sense of humor, recalled her sister, Dorothy Benedict. "She would tell people we were heiresses to Ponds Cold Cream," Benedict said with a laugh. "But we weren't really related."

She attended several boarding schools in the East and the West, and spent two years studying at Smith College in Massachusetts. In 1924 she left college to marry H. Fermor Spencer Church, who was a faculty member at her father's school.

In her early married years she was the only faculty wife at the school. Her father had retired to live in Santa Fe, and had hired a man named A.J. Connell to run the school. An avid rider and lover of mountain trails, Church was often in disagreement with Connell as to the proper behavior of a young faculty wife. And he often made his disapproval of her actions clear to her, according to her son Hugh Church. But his criticism was not enough to make her change her ways.

In the years leading up to the Second World War, Church was not only a mother and a wife, but also a successful writer who required her own privacy to do her work, her son said. "At the ranch she had a cabin on the edge of a canyon that she retreated to, to do her work," he recalled.

Her first book of poetry, "Foretaste," was published in 1933 by the Rydal Press in Santa Fe. "Familiar Journey," her second book of poems, followed in 1936, also published by Rydal Press.

"She was always torn between the practical things and the poet in her— always struggling between those two things," recalled Corina Santistevan, who had been her friend since 1946. "She lived many lives and related to many things. She was always curious, like a child. Every stone she had to feel, to touch, to pick up and weigh."

Although Los Alamos was a small town, it saw more and more visitors as the 1940s approach[ed]. One sojourner, Edith Warner, eventually became a permanent resident. She lived several miles south of town alongside the Rio Grande, in the small house that served as a train station and later as a teahouse serving many of the scientists and their families during the war years. It was eventually depicted in Church's book.

"It was Edith Warner in her little house by the bridge on the road to Los Alamos who saw it all happen," Church wrote, referring to the changes brought by the government scientists, in "The House at Otowi Bridge," which has become a Southwestern classic.

These changes were visited suddenly on the remote village of fewer than 200 inhabitants. In December 1942, a year after the United States entered World War II, Church and her family were informed that the school and their home were being taken over by the government in order to carry out a highly secret wartime project. Only 2 ½ years later, the Manhattan Project, under the direction of J. Robert Oppenheimer, would succeed with the world's first nuclear explosion at Trinity, a site in southern New Mexico. Weeks later atomic bombs would be dropped on Hiroshima and Nagasaki in Japan.

At the time, because her husband was a physics teacher Church suspected the nature of the scientific work being carried out by the government. But for her, immediately, it was an expulsion from paradise. And it forced her and her family to move to Taos, then to California, and finally again to Taos, where her husband tried unsuccessfully to open a school much like the one abandoned in Los Alamos. In 1960 the family settled in Santa Fe.

The knowledge of what Los Alamos had turned into haunted Church for the rest of her life, her sister commented. Church first expressed her outrage at the bomb in "Ultimatum for Man," a book of poetry published in 1946. However, as the years passed her outlook mellowed. After writing "The House at Otowi Bridge," she turned to writing about life, love and fate, often expressing her themes by drawing images from nature.

Throughout her life Church was constantly exploring the world, and she chose friends who were diverse in age, profession and race, recalled Santistevan. "They reflected her life," she commented.

Church had a great love for the ancestral home of the Indians in the Jemez Mountains, and had an abiding interest in all Native Americans and their lore. She particularly loved the mythical Indian character, Coyote, who could be blamed for any mishaps. "He's a trickster. He makes me lose things, forget," she said in an interview several years ago.

"Last Tuesday [before her death] when we spoke, I had a coyote story I thought Peggy might be interested in," Santistevan said. "She wanted to know who wrote it. I said that a New Yorker had written it, and we both laughed."

"She was a religious person in the universal sense," added Santistevan.

Church's husband died in 1975. A year later she published "New and Selected Poems," and in 1978 she published "The Ripened Fields: Fifteen Sonnets of a Marriage." In 1981 she published "A Rustle of Angels."

In 1984 she received a Governor's Award for her contributions to art. And a year later she published her last book of poetry, "Birds of Daybreak: Landscapes and Elegies."

For many years Church lived in a house on Camino Ranchitos, and about a year ago she moved into an apartment in the El Castillo Retirement Residences.

As she grew older Church developed a fondness for collecting native plants and rocks for her garden, remembered her friend and neighbor Mary Miam. Several days before Church's death, Miam brought her one of the rocks she treasured the most from the garden of her former home. "Her poetry reminded me of the rocks and flowers in her garden: delicate yet strong," Miam said.

Over the last several years Church developed allergies to many things in her environment, according to her son Hugh. She was also upset and frustrated at slowly losing her senses of sight and hearing. "She was so dependent upon her senses," remarked her son.

She was a "card-carrying" member of the Hemlock Society, which counsels people with terminal illnesses about suicide, her son Hugh said. Church often talked about how to deal with people as they got old and infirm, according to her son. "She put herself to sleep," he said, referring to her death.

She is survived by three sons, Theodore Church, Allen Church and Hugh Church, all of Albuquerque; a sister, Dorothy Benedict of Oregon; five grandchildren and three great-grand children.

The New Mexican, Sunday, October 26, 1986
by
The New Mexican Staff

Margaret "Peggy" Pond Church, a poet and author whose works recalled early days in northern New Mexico, died Thursday at home. She was 82.

Her father, Ashley Pond II, founded the Los Alamos Ranch School in 1916. The school became the site of the Manhattan Project, where the first atomic weapons were made.

Church's poems and books recalled growing up on Pajarito Plateau, a volcanic ash formation that includes the Los Alamos mesa, which became known as "The Hill."

In a 1981 interview with *The New Mexican*, she said she spent a lot of time outdoors and became an ardent lover of nature.

In *A Lament on Tsankawi Mesa*, she wrote about the changes that her much-loved hill had undergone:

> What has changed?
> Is it I who have changed?
> The light-footed child I was no longer answers
> the exuberant life has dwindled…
> Giant machines with an evil eye
> spread themselves over the mesa;…

Pond's *House at Otowi Bridge* told the Los Alamos story through the life of one woman, Edith Warner, who was a station master for the Denver and Rio Grande narrow-guage train. Her last book, *Birds of Daybreak*, was a collection of poetry printed in 1985.

Church was born in Watrous Dec. 1, 1903 to the late Ashley and Hazel Hallett Pond. Her husband of 50 years, Fermor S. Church, and her brother, Dr. Ashley Pond III, both died earlier.

She is survived by three sons, Theodore, Allen and Hugh, all of Albuquerque; six grandchildren; three great-grandchildren; and her sister, Dorothy Benedict of Glendale, Oregon.

A memorial service will be held by the Santa Fe Friends Meeting. The McGee Memorial is handling funeral arrangements.

Memorial donations may be made to The School of American Research in Santa Fe, St. John's College, or the Los Alamos Historical Society's Peggy Pond Church Endowment Fund.

V

EDITION OF 1936

Familiar Journey

FAMILIAR JOURNEY

Peggy Pond Church

WRITERS' EDITIONS · SANTA FE · NEW MEXICO

Acknowledgment is made to "Poetry"
for permission to print certain of these poems

This book is published by Writers' Editions, a cooperative group of
writers living in the Southwest, who believe that regional publica-
tion will foster the growth of American literature

CONTENTS

Part II

THE SISTER'S SONG

My brother who seeks the talking bird
gave me a jewel and a laughing word.
My brother who seeks the flowering tree
left his house and his lands with me,
but my brother who seeks the water of life
left me nought but his silver knife.
If the blade grows dull, if the blade grows dim
I will know some evil has come to him
and I must search the land and sea
to find my brother and set him free.

The house and lands are very fair;
the jewel is a lustre in my hair,
it is carved and set with a cunning art,
but I wear the knife against my heart.

PART 1

ON A MORNING

On a morning
when the mountains were walls of fire
and the clouds like
curled smoke,
the blossoms of many trees were
flames of another color.
I stood with you
breast to breast,
pressed to you in an embrace without pressure,
your mouth upon my mouth,
out of us both, out of both our hearts a flame springing,
separately rooted,
arching over us,
merging into one flame
streaming upward,
absorbing quietly
the fire of the mountains,
mingling with itself
the burning blossoms.

CARVED IN IVORY

Carve this in ivory,
delicate hand of a dead craftsman!
Rise from the grave.
Stand upright,
bone upon unaccustomed bone.
Take shape, oh dust!
Remember, oh atoms of dust, the shape of the body.
Become a hand to carve this moment in ivory
so that it shall last forever,
leaf-shape, tree-root,
poise of a finger,
miniature pattern of flowers upon the garment,
even the shape the wind takes in the branches,
and the shape of love transfixed on the face of
        the lover.

ALCHEMY

Strange when the essence of flowers
is indistinguishable from music
Strange when music
blossoms like a flower
that can be seen as the blind see, only with the fingers.
Strange when the body
turns into bread and wine.

This is an alchemy
of which no alchemist would ever dream.
To change flowers for music,
music for flowers,
stars for fingers,
body to bread,
bread into wine,
wine into god,
everything at last into love.

AFTER THE RAIN

After the rain the earth lies back in sunlight,
her lovely limbs relaxed, her breasts quiescent,
her long hair spread upon the wind like perfume.
After the rain the earth becomes a woman
a lover can lie at peace with, becomes a woman
who holds in her hands the weightless arch of the rainbow.
She lies with her eyes half-closed. She lies half-dreaming.
She lies like a swimmer half-submerged in sunlight.

HUMMING BIRDS

And I have watched the humming-birds coming
all morning to the honeysuckle vine.
Every flower
is beautiful and the birds take
sweetness from every flower.
I lie here in the morning sun,
the sun that finds me through the honeysuckle leaves,
and I think of the sweetness my heart has,
and the sweetness of many hearts.
And I am glad of the sun
and the sap running through the branches of the honeysuckle,
and of the birds that come, so many of them,
to the unceasing fountain of these blossoms.

WE SPOKE OF LOVE

We spoke of love by every usual name.
We said it was a bird, a song, a light,
the bread and wine of life, a cloud, a flame,
the scent of flowers upon the air at night.
Music we said it was, heard in a dream
no mortal might remember or forget.
It was the moving air, the flowing stream.
It was a sun that never rose nor set.
With countless names we sought to bind love fast.
We saw it float from every subtle snare,
leaving but shadow in each shape at last,
each tangible shape we built for it to wear.
At last we ceased to speak. Then love became
the silence in our hearts and bore no name.

LOVE WAS A BIRD

Love was a bird we found with faltering wing.
Most pitifully it answered to our call.
We held it in our hands. It could not sing.
We felt its breast with terror rise and fall.
We warmed it on our hearts. It breathed again.
Its wings moved soft between your heart and mine.
From our own lips it took the golden grain,
turning each kiss into its bread and wine.
When morning came, renewed and fortified,
in our embracing arms the great wings stirred.
We could not keep love captive if we tried.
We loosed our hands. We saw the shining bird
spread wide its wings and soar in ecstasy
forever wild and beautiful and free.

FOR RAIN

Let there be now
this day and this night of healing,
for you, for me, for the earth, for all who need it;
the quietness of rain to rest in,
rain on the roof,
rain on the leaves of the orchards,
rain on the round surface of water in the garden,
rain that shuts each dwelling in a shell of quietness,
a little cocoon of silence.
And let there be peace for us both, for the earth,
for all who need it,
the peace that lovers have at last and sleeping
shoulder to shoulder, oblivious of passion.

OF FRAGMENTS THAT REMAINED

The need, when I have been with you, to be more loving,
you and I who have broken the bread of life together—
"And they did eat and were all filled: and there was taken up
of fragments that remained to them twelve baskets."
The world is hungry.
The world is full of miracles.
I go from you with the fragments of love in twelve baskets.
It is enough, I think, to feed the whole world!

HEART'S BROTHER

Yesterday
I walked in the crowd.
I touched the hands of many.
I hid myself in words like a forest of aspens
twinkling and glittering as the wind stirs them,
and all the time in my heart this secret singing
like a crystal flower of a spring under leaves in the forest—
Yonder, unknown to any but my own heart,
my brother walks,
my heart's brother.

COMPANIONED

Companioned by my lord, the sun,
companioned by my sister, moon,
and by the unbeseeching wind,
and water's almost soundless tune;
companioned by my brother, fire,
and by the flowering candlelight,
all worldless things that make me kin
and bid me welcome here tonight,
though you, my love, come not at all,
by love I am companioned still,
the love that shines from every leaf,
that silent streams from every hill.
My own heart shines and quietly,
whether you come, or not at all,
your love speaks in all wordless things,
and like your touch the slow leaves fall.

AND I IMAGINED

I stood at the end of the ski trail
on the level ground, alone and
with all my blood leaping
at the touch of the cold air,
alone and thinking that
if you were standing there,
if you were waiting for me
I should be folded in your arms now.

And I imagined that you were there
and I was bringing you the gift of my joy.

When I lifted my head and faced the sky again
the frost had turned all the tears in my eyes
to rainbows.

AND THERE WAS LIGHT

We have climbed this hill out of a black darkness,
a maelstrom of black darkness.

And now this,
this white night,
the snow sending the moon's light back again
shining and undisturbed,
and the dark sky, blue, oh deeply blue,
bluer than ever daylight was but dark,
and the stars shining.

Standing upon this hill
and joy like a light within me,
I and the stars singing the same song,
and this light including us all.

I will soar in a moment
upon the translucent snow,
fitting my skis to the curve of the hill,
soaring as the hill curves,
cleaving moonlight,
cleaving the still air,
tracing the pattern of flight upon the smooth snow,
over the arc of the white hill.

Making a pattern of beauty
in this winter night,
making a pattern
out of the joy in my heart,
out of my love for you.

TO BE SUNG IN WINTER

This weight of white, these plumèd wings,
this feather-breasted, ancient bird
comes down upon us like a dream,
comes on us like a blessed word.

The fir tree bends its archèd branch
low to the ground, oh low and still,
and not a wind can pierce this web,
and not a sound come nigh this hill.

Now you and I in folded sleep
lie breast to breast and quietly,
your hands like wings against my hair,
your knee above my naked knee.

And here we sleep as children sleep
unwakened yet from the dark womb;
thou, brother to my heart, and I,
your sister in a single doom.

The pattern of this love is laid
so deep in blood, so deep in bone,
we lie enchanted in one dream,
we call one single heart our own.

And we shall wake when term is spent,
and we shall rise and softly go,
and we shall tread as angels tread
across the still, unstainèd snow.

NO OTHER

What has flesh and blood to do
with this white world shaped of unbreathing crystal,
these mountains like an ethereal cold breath
blown on the colder sky?
Yes, we saw the red sun go down
and the white, frost-like wafer of the moon come up,
but our hearts were still sheathed in ice like the buds of the roses,
and I knew of no way to invoke the miracle
that would make a rose blossom in winter
or warm the cold snow,
or hasten the season for lovers who share no other
home than the green earth.

AGAIN THE FLOWERING

Hardly now can I wait
for summer and again the flowering,
the sun on the path between the willows, on the deep clover,
earth praising the sun
in her many-leafed, her myriad-petalled voices,
and a bird's shadow like the arc of a flower fallen
across the bright sky.

Hardly now can I wait
to hold the sunlight again in my arms, I naked
and shoulders pressed to the warm earth,
holding the sun there,
the great sun drowsy and drowned like a bee drowned
in the deep fountain of a golden poppy.

WINTER LANDSCAPE

These bare trees
have peace in the grey quiet of their branches.
They are wiser than I.
They know how to accept winter.
They do not regret the feverish ecstasy of autumn.
They are not impatient for the radiance of spring.
They know they cannot hurry the seasons.
Upon the sky their shapes are effortlessly beautiful.
They stand quietly, letting the wind have its way with them.
Beholding them this mind is quieted,
this heart ceases to struggle and cry out for summer.

THIS OCEAN

All day we watched the ocean
heaping its white, incredibly brief blossoms
over the agony-veined, dark granite:
all day the green sea-water
thrusting into the rock clefts.

Seals basked,
barking at tide's edge,
swam, elusive as thought,
under the fluid marble
surface of deep water.

Cypress
more ancient than memory
absorbed us into shadow.

I saw dead girls
bruise their white breasts
on the indifferent rock,
sea-sharpened, crystal, harder than diamond:
their long hair
netted the pale tide.

Darkness came down:
the gaunt sea-vultures
roosted, red-beaked
in the bleak rock.

I dared not touch you
with word or weight of finger:
your own gods claimed you, the elemental granite
bare at your heart's core.

Now I must take this ocean
into my own heart or be taken by it,
going down into it, naked and voiceless and
torn by the rocks like the drowned girls.

THE KNIFE I THRUST

Not one cloud in the sky,
and the sun is golden on the pine needles,
the sun is golden,
and I lie on the ground face down,
face down in the brown needles
press my breast upon the pine needles
wounding myself on their sharpness.
I bare my back, naked to the sun at noonday,
praying him to wound me that I may forget all other wounds,
but it avails me nothing.
I can still feel the knife twisting in my heart,
the sharp knife turning,
the knife I thrust into the heart of beloved.

OH MERCIFUL LORD

Oh merciful Lord,
I pray you for my beloved,
my beloved who said:
"This is a beautiful sword wherewith you have wounded me.
I shall cherish the sharpness of it in my heart forever."

THERE WAS NOTHING

There was nothing I could do for my beloved,
and so I put my arms around a child who was crying,
and kissed one who was hungry for my kiss,
and spoke to another who was lonely.

AND IN THE LATE AFTERNOON

And in the late afternoon
I go down to the edge of the canyon and watch the swallows,
and wonder why all the birds seem to fly westward
up the pathway of the canyon at evening.

And the slow rhythm of the wind
and the slow rhythm of the swallows flying
and the slow rhythm of the lengthening shadows
quiet me at last,
and I forget that I am mortal
and torn with mortal griefs.

I LAY AT NIGHT

I lay at night in the dark bed weeping for my beloved,
and the stars were caught like fireflies in the
                              weaving
branches of the honeysuckle.
The scent of the olives was an uncomplaining sorrow
that spread in the night.
At first the wind was silent.

At midnight the tempo changed.
The music of the wind became allegro agitato.
The wind climbed the dark sky, marching.

There came to me then, out of the troubled darkness
one who had been walking alone in the late night,
                              weeping,
and because my heart was heavy with love and nowhere
                              to shed it,
I put my grief from me.
I gathered him in my arms.
I held him to me,
and I saw as though my eyes that had been blind were opened
that he whom I held on my heart was my beloved.
It was he for whom I had lain in the dark bed,
                              alone and weeping.

NO ARMOR

I drew my hand from out the dead's cold hand
and shuddering fled, now that his need was done,
back to the living, to the blossoming land,
to the quiet mountains, patient in the sun;
but found no comfort there, but found no rest,
no armor against death. My sudden need
was for your living hand upon my breast,
your warmth to warm me and your lips to heed
the ache of mine that had seen lips grow taut,
clenched firm upon the hard-relinquished breath,
forgetful then that flesh had once been hot
and eager and oblivious of death.
Oh hold me on your living heart and strong
for immortality is sad and long.

LIKE LITTLE CHILDREN LOST

Like little children lost we make brave sound.
We loudly boast that we are not afraid.
So long as sunlight warms the trackless ground
who cares if Death lurks in the distant shade?
We fill the frightened silences with song,
with manful words mislead our enemy.
He will not be so stern if we are strong.
He scorns those most who bend the coward knee.
But when before us on the sands we tread
we find Death's mighty print and the torn feather
stripped from his quarry, vanished now and dead,
we tremble. We draw close to one another.
What though our souls are brave and know not fear?
Still must this flesh cry out when Death is near.

FORSYTHIA

The pale forsythia's soundless bells
yellow upon the unleafed stem.
Oh winter-frozen heart, put forth
your long-quenched flowers to answer them.
Wait not for sun. Wait not for leaf.
Wait for no certain signs of Spring.
The roots of the forsythia knew
before the robin's listening wing.
The waiting song within the root
leapt like a flame the wind compels
along the frozen stem until
the sudden branch was bloomed with bells.
Shake off, oh heart, this chill despair
nor doubt that gods walk still with men.
Behold the miracle renewed,
the barren rod in flower again.

THERE WAS NO FEAR NOW

Before I entered the dark wood
I went to my beloved. I said:
The way is lonely ; the night is dark ;
and I am afraid.
I am afraid of the darkness.

My beloved answered me with not one kiss.
He did not touch me with eyes or lips or hands.
He opened his heart. He gave me a flower from it.
I took it in silence. I entered the lonely land.

I found there was no peril that could touch me.
The sharp thorns budded. They changed in one instant to flowers.
Tawny beasts knelt at my feet. They licked my feet softly.
The stars were watchmen changing every hour.

I crossed the wood safely. At last I met my beloved.
I laid myself like a shadow against his heart.
The flower took root in his heart. It grew. It blossomed.
There was no fear now upon earth to hold us apart.

AMFORTAS

I mounted up a secret stair.
I crossed the room to you.
I saw a wound upon your breast,
*   a wound that grew.*

You folded me within your arms.
The wound began to bleed.
The wound was red upon your breast,
*   ah red indeed.*

The stain came off upon my hand,
the warm, the flowing stain.
Alas, said I, does he not know
*   it bleeds again?*

I held my hand for you to see
how bright your heart's blood flowed.
You smiled. You kissed me then. You said,
*   The wound is old.*

I knew then what it was had made
the wound upon your breast,
that it was love and only love
*   could give it rest.*

Oh mystery! Oh holy wound!
Oh ancient hidden pain!
Only the spear that pierced the heart
*   can heal the heart again!*

My fear and wonder left me then,
my heart's own swift alarms.
I stood for longer than a dream
quiet in your arms.

ANNUNCIATION

Visions attended her. She moved in dream.
Dark clouds withheld their storm until she passed.
She watched the hills dissolve into a flame.
She saw dry rivers deep with rain at last.

The hills assumed a strange, ancestral form.
They shone in living light upon the sky.
Down the wet, shining road she moved in dream.
She saw the long spears of the lightning fly.

There was no darkness could affright her now.
There was no light too sharp for her to bear.
She moved in dream. Her own heart like a cloud
quickened with light as though a child lay there.

The hands of love were warm upon her hands.
The breast of love against her breast lay bright.
She moved in dream, quiet and unafraid
as though she were impregnate of all light.

EAST OF THE SUN AND WEST OF THE MOON

In the deep of night I lighted my candle and saw you sleeping,
beautiful as a hero, as a young god, as my beloved,
frank in your maleness, acquiescent to your beauty,
lying there lightly in pale light as a child lies.

I bent over you marvelling,
I bent over you in exaltation and in sorrow
knowing this for the moment out of fairy-tale
when the maiden first sees her love in his true shape, sleeping
and spills the tallow of her candle on his shoulder
so that he wakes and vanishes, and she must seek him
through the inevitable seven years of legend.

She must wander, questioning, through the wide world,
must cross the burning ploughshares, the fierce glass mountain,
and wake him from his sleep, and make him know her
forever as his true love.

In the deep of night I leaned over you, holding my candle
in terror and awe of this quest, this quest that must lead me
east of the sun and west of the moon until I find you
beautiful as a hero, as a young god, as my beloved
standing before me forever in your true shape.

THE DAYLIGHT COMES

The daylight comes while I lie watching you,
watching the morning brighten on your face,
each curve and line my midnight fingers knew
that traced them in the dark as blind girls trace
a dear, familiar lineament. The day
shows me your face as once in candle-glow
Psyche saw Love before he fled away
up a dark heaven where she could not go.
Ah do not wake. Embrace me in your dream.
We could but weep and part if you should wake.
A sword between us is this morning gleam,
the sword between all lovers. Do not wake,
lest looking in your eyes I lose the will
to leave you now, and tearless, dreaming still.

I, LIKE AN EXILE

I, like an exile who must sail at dawn,
am borne from you upon the tide of day.
The shore's thin crescent narrows and is gone,
veiled now in mist is all the lovely bay;
veiled in swift tears my last faint glimpse of shore,
and blurred with tears the image of the land
imprinted on my heart, the light it wore,
the light upon your face, your lifted hand.
Though the great sun, I know, is still the same,
and shines in other lands on hills as fair,
and other faces sometimes wear a flame,
and these bright flowers will blossom anywhere,
all dear, familiar shapes can now remind
me only of this land left far behind.

VALE

I opened the door, though I knew I would not find you.
You had gone without making a sound, without saying a word.
The air was as still as though you had never passed there,
still as dark water by the wind unstirred.

Only my heart still trembled, still remembered,
as water trembles in rings where a bird has flown,
a bird that drifted an instant against its shadow,
breast upon imaged breast, as quiet as stone,

as light as cloud, and then at last has vanished
leaving no trace behind, leaving no sound,
only the ripples that widen and spread in silence,
that die in a silver wave along the ground.

There was no more than this for me to remember.
The leaves hung quiet that had lately seen you pass.
I could not find, though I searched the night forever,
one print of your foot left warm upon the grass.

PART II

FAMILIAR JOURNEY

Back and forth on the same road
and the same hills.
I and the seasons going back and forth
on the same road; the orchards blossoming,
ripening their fruit, and the harvest gathered.
A new house is built and an old one
crumbles. In the late nights
one window is sometimes lighted.
Who watches in silence
while an old man dies or a child is being born?
I and the stars go past
again and again on the same road.

The dark nights and the bright ones,
the summer days
with the clouds blossoming above the mountains,
tremendous flowers, white, and sheathed in purple
like the flowers of yucca;
and the meadow larks
with a song as cool as the fields of green alfalfa;
the cottonwood tree
at the curve of the ditch near Pojuaque
where the old men sit all day
and the young girls at night with their lovers,
the old tree that remembers
more than the oldest man in that village remembers
and that dies slowly now, withdrawing its shadow
a little every year.

And the luminous valley
where nothing grows but color,
blues, lavenders, violets,
and all the shades of rose seen in a sunset;

49

the long bluff like a wave,
a wave the color of a cloud at sunset,
a wave that never breaks,
transfixed forever at the moment of its breaking,
and the sharp spires like the bending crest of the wave;
the hills that go naked always to the sun,
naked to starlight,
clothing themselves in no shadow,
the remnants of ancient valleys,
fragments of canyon walls the wind and weather
have not destroyed yet,
secret valleys
only the sun and the wind know.

I going back and forth on the same road
as if it were another body that contained me:
and the great storms, the afternoons of sunlight,
the dark nights,
the mountains that are a flame on one horizon,
and the mountains like a blue, an incandescent shadow
rimming the west;

Familiar journey,
and the years of a life,
the happenings of a life
along this road like remembered hills,
like the valleys.

THIS HAVE I SEEN

This have I seen in my dreams;
a white flower floating upon dark water,
dark water that mirrors nothing,
that contains only itself,
no image of starlight,
no hills reflected,
only this flower into which all light is gathered,
the light distilled from the dark water,
the light distilled from the dark heaven,
this light consuming nothing, illuminating nothing,
only itself, motionless, golden-hearted, floating
under dark heaven on the surface of dark water.

THE DARK FISH

This was a path she knew:
footprints more ancient than memory
set in stone,
set in stone to be followed only in the half glance,
and the feet, bare as in childhood, remembering blindly,
running shyly and traceless as the wind runs
(lest she be followed, lest the heavy of foot should follow.)

And here is a pool the tide and the rains have forgotten
set in the cleft of a high rock,
the dark fish moving
lithe and translucent in the clear water,
delicate-finned and
swifter than fallen shadow,
shining with the incipience of color,
wild and live and
breath-takingly beautiful.

She watches them for the infinity of a held breath
and goes again quickly,
trembling in her flight lest any should have followed,
lest this secret be ever discovered.

YELLOW POPLAR

No snow has fallen.
Should the snow fall tonight,
think, tomorrow, of the pale blue shadow
on white snow of this golden poplar,
of the gold leaves blowing
like stars, a thousand of them, falling
across blue daylight;
beneath the blue sky the white snow
starred with the gold leaves.

This tree is more beautiful
than anything I have ever seen in autumn.
It is as though
it were rooted in the sky, not earth,
as though its sap were sunlight.

The color of these leaves is like no other color
but that of the yellow full moon in September,
newly risen, tangent still with the horizon.
This poplar is colored like a yellow moon.
It shines as brightly.
It is like a lantern in the sky lighting the dark pines.

AUTUMN DUSK

Over the hill's dark edge
the road curves.
Yellow gathers like a cloud at the bend beyond the river,
rushes toward us up the roadside.

Color of trees, autumnal, moving in a new dimension,
forward in space, and the wave breaks as the car leaps through it.
The oiled ribbon of dark road
unwinds in yellow margins.

Motion of machinery,
hurrying pistons in rhythmical vertical descension,
wheel circumference revolving on the hard road.
The season draws its slow arc on the earth's shell.
The arc of sunset
widens like a stain in the pale sky.

Oh luminous evening
cleft at the core like a silver knife through a fruit's heart,
the two halves opening backward.
The core is motionless,
is speed quiescent at the heart of motion.
We move like an arrow bearing our swiftness with us.
The moon comes up out of last light and follows us slowly.

MIDWINTER NIGHT

Snow lashing against the windows
in a cascade, in a white mist.
Wind grips night in its sharp teeth,
shakes night by the teeth like a fierce dog.
The mother wakes and goes about her house softly,
bends over the children, touches their warm hands,
encloses them with her love as once in her body,
feels herself never so much the mother as when she
           holds them in safety
on this fierce night in the midst of wild wind
and the white snow flying.

WATCHING MOONRISE

Leaning on the window, alone and watching the
anonymous lights of the city.
The moon will rise soon. This is that
silver-sharpened hour of darkness before the
moon comes.

Dogs bark,
sharp and barbaric, uttering their cries from
backyard to alley to dark street,
they who are alien to the moon,
troubled, they know not why, at her coming,
unleashing their voices only in the half-light
of transient shadow that eases them briefly
of moon magic.

I who am sleepless, leaning on the sill of the window,
invisible to the city, watching the noise and the thrust of it,
alone and unsurprised as the calm moon if you should
walk out of the darkness,
hold me for one eternal instant and wordless
vanish into moonrise,

watching the mountain press on the edge of bright moon
in eternal acquiescence

DOWN TO THE WATER

I went down to the water,
down among dead leaves,
among tangled branches
to the edge of the water
seeking and calling.
It was you I went seeking.
It was you I must find there.

No sign of Spring yet.
The branches were barren,
no light within leaf buds.
Cold shone the water,
motionless, crystalline.
Slowly I went down,
groping and stumbling.

You called me. I answered.
In this dream it was twilight,
and I hung my one garment
on a branch at the lake's edge.
I saw you there waiting
waist deep in water
naked and shining.

The water received me.
It drew me toward you,
warm as in summer,
limpid, translucent.
Our bodies' pale shadows
shimmered and trembled
upon that clear water.

Nearby were cities
that emptied their sewage
into this deep lake.
How then, I wondered,
shone it so purely,
so uncontaminate
of any foulness?

In the ravines I had
crossed through to come there
old cans lay rotting,
the cities' excreta ;
steel twisted, distorted,
machinery ruined and
thrown on the dump heap.

And yet how cleanly
this water received us.
I gave myself utterly
up to the dream then,
wondered no longer but
waded to touch you,
found you, embraced you,

wet thigh to wet thigh.
I leaned on the water.
Your hands upheld me.
You carried me swiftly
whither I knew not.
Finally you laid me
in shallow water.

Wet then and shining
merged we together
becoming one shadow
within the water,
till the dream vanished
as rings upon water
widen and vanish.

CHRIST'S BIRTHDAY

Remembering the light
and the angel's thunder
Mary smiles now
in relief and wonder.

This child is a babe
like any other.
God is a baby
needing His mother.

A stable folds him,
a place to sleep
warmed by the quiet
sweet breath of sheep.

The cattle stand
mild-eyed and knowing
to see this woman
with her young breasts flowing,

to see this small thing
nuzzle her breast
helpless and hungry
as the least or best.

What shall I bring him?
What will he treasure
who has had king's gifts
and gold without measure?

The arrow-pointed
print of a deer,
traced upon snowfall
light and clear;

luminous pallor
of winter grasses
whose seeds are winged feathers
when the least wind passes:

a cool smooth twig
from the wild choke-cherry,
and the velvet sheen
on a juniper berry.

ANN

Ann
is pixie-dark;
looks out like a pixie under dark hair;
might be taken for a
witch's tangle-haired daughter;
has a knowledge she won't disclose of
witch-secrets;
plays with human children
a little solemnly,
a little condescending.

Suddenly forgets her
witchness, pixieness,
tosses hoyden heels;
goes modern, goes tomboy,
all but the tremulous
deep voice like the sound of heartbreak
or green sea-water,
or wind at twilight
swirling down over a mountain.

TUMBLEWEED

Whit
moves down the path
blown by the wind like tumbleweed
a little to one side,
a little to the other;
marches on legs spread wide apart,
holds his hands in front of him
lightly,
lays his hands in the wind's hands
and runs.

Red sweater,
brown suit,
brown eyes,
very dark brown lashes,
hair the color of yellow grass
turning brown in autumn,
brown hair, tangled hair,
forehead-hiding hair.

Puts his hands in the wind's hands and runs;
falls, betrayed;
gets up, laughs a little, runs on,
blows a little to this side, to that
like tumbleweed.

BROWN BOY

The brown boy
wet with the raindrops
lies on the warm grass,
lies at ease beautiful
in the sunlight,
beautiful in every pose he takes;
sprawling full length
wet head on curved arms,
all long slim brown curves,
and the sex like a furled flower,
sheathed still, unblossomed,
lying on curled leaves.
He turns on his face,
rears up slightly
on firm bent elbows.
The buttocks are small
twin mounds, the brown back
slopes in a heart-catching curve
to the brown shoulders.
He is all grace and
incredible wild beauty.
Is there no way to
keep him from eating
the serpent's apple?
To keep him from knowing
that he is naked,
that he is beautiful?
Is there no place in the
world for a brown boy
to be beautiful forever,
just as the sun is,
the sun who asks nothing
because of his shining?

FOR THE LAST-BORN

Sitting
quiet for only one moment,
in the slow, vine-mottled afternoon sunlight,
small and fragile-boned,
under the soft, the innocent, the unturbulent flesh,
man-child, and smallest, and the
last-born!

Crawl naked in the sun, feeling the wind on your body
feeling the cool grass, soft and lightly springing
under knees and questing hands.
Crouch in the grass and laugh at the feel of muscles
rippling from toes to fingers. Disregard nothing,
no small detail of living,
no movement of sunlight
upon the ground escaping a leaf's shadow,
nor the light sound of spray
tossed from the garden hose and falling in rainbows
of music on the flat leaves of the honeysuckle.

Pull yourself up by that branch
and stand precariously a moment, laughing in triumph.
A wooden clothespin
is treasure enough for you this afternoon, a wooden clothespin
smooth and curved and fitting your hand exactly,
can be rattled or rolled or waved or
used to pound with,
is all your world for the moment.

A humming bird
poised in the air before a nectar-brimming
flower, fans the light into a miniature tumult
then, while you stare, entranced and wondering,

vanishes.
The pine tree sheds its flowers
in a brown shower, small worm-shaped thudding blossoms
rough to the fingers, and a cone drops
with a staccato sound.

Now small and tender
relaxed at last and yielding
for a little moment all your weight to the arm that holds you
warm against my breast, naked and
sun-fragrant and the soft, indefinite
hair blown in brief curls,
for this little moment
rest in my love as for a slow nine months in the untroubled
dark haven of my body.

Your world is still a world all sound and color
and moving brightness. Why did I bring you
little and defenceless,
into this world of living? I who know now
that death has cruel and many bitter weapons.
Oh my last-born,
fast in this trap now,
this trap baited with love, baited with moments of beauty,
love that lasts only an instant, one burning instant
out of a night's long darkness, beauty "like honey
laid on the sharp, the inescapable thorns of living."
What is this world
you and I too must live in until death frees us?
What is this joy that invincibly hungers for
living?

ENCHANTED MESA

Hard to climb:
the slow talus
yielding under the bent step:
the cleft in the rock where
the wind leaps
upward like chill flame:
swallows screaming.

Earth's weight
drags at the belly.
The heart soars.
Torn between
earth and clean air
we hang
clenched in hard rock.

Hand over hand now:
the blood roars
in the reluctant throat veins.
Do not look downward
onto the warm plain,
the level, the acquiescent
safe earth.

These perpendicular
weather-fractured cliffs of
sandstone intercept the
sharp sky.
The complacent
mind drags at the
winged heel.

But the bright edge
finally triumphs.
We stand fast,
erect in wind's path.
The waves of
time beat on the
sheer rock.

Swallows
protest our coming.
go past us like
arrows from a tense bow,
curved flight,
cleaving wind with
their sharp cries.

An hour on this
mesa escapes time.
Humanity vanishes,
becomes an unheard procession
on remote roads. Only the strong
skeletal firmness of earth holds
sky on its shoulders.

Holds us also
that which we strove against
in climbing.
The heart soars
lifted upon its own roots.
Enchanted Mesa—
a winged rock rooted in the
spent plain.

AUTUMN EVENING

What does a woman think of
sitting at her window in the quiet hour,
the sad hour of evening, the hour of the yellow
leaves falling,
the hour of the earth circling into darkness and the
last sun ebbing?

The gay pink of the larkspur has faded.
Chrysanthemums lean heavily, bowed with too much
burden of yellow.
The drowned leaves have silvered the still pool like a
mirror.
Only the mountains at the world's edge burn still
with sunlight,
a wall of fire lifting out of the dark earth.

And I am sad without sadness
at this end of daylight and of summer,
unreluctant as earth in the long gestation of winter,
the earth turning against the cold sky
heavy with springtime.

www.ingramcontent.com/pod-product-compliance
Lightning Source LLC
Chambersburg PA
CBHW022014080426
42733CB00007B/599